O9-ABI-802

Rookie
Read-About® Holidays

Election Day

By Patricia J. Murphy

Consultants
Nanci Vargus, Ed.D.
Primary Multiage Teacher
Decatur Township Schools, Indianapolis, Indiana

Katharine A. Kane, Reading Specialist
Former Language Arts Coordinator
San Diego County Office of Education

Children's Press®
A Division of Scholastic Inc.
New York   Toronto   London   Auckland   Sydney
Mexico City   New Delhi   Hong Kong
Danbury, Connecticut

Designer: Herman Adler Design
Photo Researcher: Caroline Anderson
The photo on the cover shows children voting in a classroom.

Library of Congress Cataloging-in-Publication Data

Murphy, Patricia J., 1963-
 Election day / by Patricia J. Murphy.
  p. cm. — (Rookie read-about holidays)
 Includes index.
 Summary: Explains the importance of voting, different methods of voting,
 and how voting helps us take part in our government.
  ISBN 0-516-22663-0 (lib. bdg.) 0-516-27488-0 (pbk.)
  1. Elections—United States—History—Juvenile literature. 2. Election
 Day—History—Juvenile literature. [1. Elections. 2. Election Day.] I. Title.
 II. Series.
 JK1978 .M868 2002
 324.6'3'0973—dc21
                                        2002005488

CHILDREN'S PRESS, AND ROOKIE READ-ABOUT®,
and associated logos are trademarks and or registered trademarks
of Grolier Publishing Co., Inc. SCHOLASTIC and associated logos
are trademarks and or registered trademarks of Scholastic Inc.

1 2 3 4 5 6 7 8 9 10 R 11 10 09 08 07 06 05 04 03 02

Do you know what an election is?

Peanut Butter
Coffee & Cream
Banana
Bubble Gum
Strawberry
Cotton Candy
Raspberry
Black Cherry

4

An election is when people get to choose, or vote. You make choices every day.

In an election, people might vote on who they want to be a leader in their town, city, or state.

Sometimes people choose what laws, or rules, everyone should follow.

In the United States, there
is a special day to vote.
It is called Election Day.

Election Day is the first
Tuesday after the first
Monday in November.

November 2002

Sunday	Monday	Tuesday	Wednesday	Thursday	Friday	Saturday
					1	2
3	4	5	6	7	8	9
10	11	12	13	14	15	16
17	18	19	20	21	22	23
24	25	26	27	28	29	30

People elect, or choose, someone to become the President of the United States every four years.

12

People have voted in elections for thousands of years.

Voting was the beginning of democracy. In a democracy, people are able to choose their leaders. The government in the United States is a democracy.

16

Only white men who owned land could vote when our country began. This small group chose the leaders for all the rest of the people.

At this time, African Americans and women were not allowed to vote. They wanted things to be fair. They worked hard to get the government to let them vote.

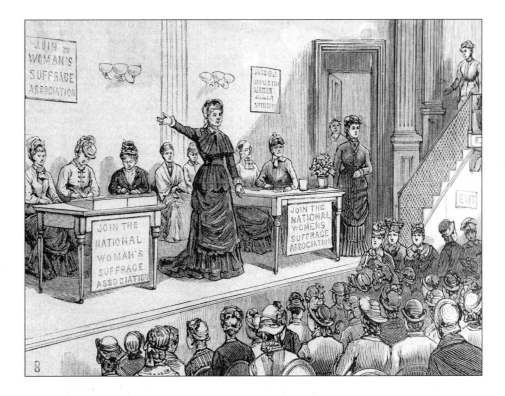

19

Now everyone has a chance to vote. You must register, or sign up, to vote in an election. You must be at least 18 years old. You must be a citizen of the United States.

People vote in their neighborhoods. They can vote in a school, library, post office, church, or home.

23

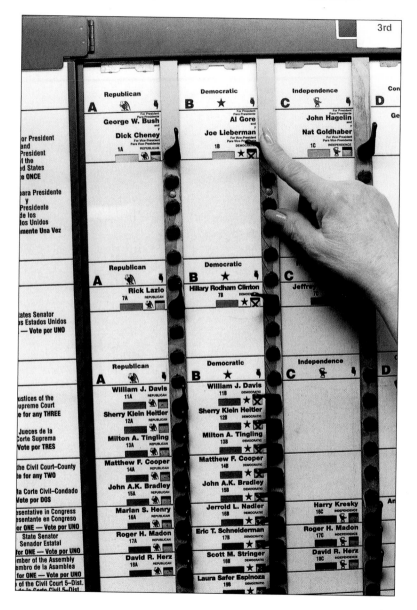

24

Many people use voting machines to vote. These machines have little metal bars next to each choice. Voters must pull the bars to make their choices.

Some people vote on paper. They use special cards called ballots. They mark their choices. Then they place their ballot in a ballot box.

27

Now it's time to count
the votes to see who
the people have chosen.

Words You Know

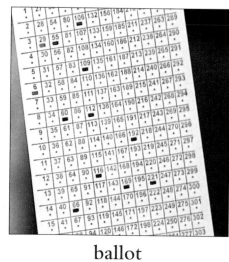

ballot

ballot box

choose

election

President of the
United States

register

vote

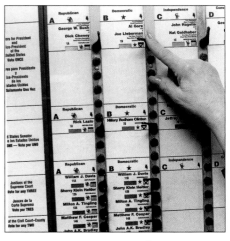

voting machine

Index

About the Author

Patricia J. Murphy writes children's storybooks, nonfiction books, early readers, and poetry. She also writes for magazines, corporations, educational publishing companies, and museums. She resides in the Northbrook, IL. Every Election Day, Patricia makes sure to cast her vote!

Photo Credits